MA

*PRODUCED BY
MADONNA AND
PATRICK LEONARD
**PRODUCED BY
MADONNA AND STEPHEN BRAY
***PRODUCED BY
MADONNA, PATRICK
LEONARD AND
STEPHEN BRAY

1. PAPA DON'T PREACH** 4:27
(Brian Elliot: Additional Lyrics by
Madonna)Elliot Music Corp.
(MCPS Ltd.)/Jacobsen Music

2. OPEN YOUR HEART* 4:1
(Madonna/Gardner Cole
Ralfelson) Warner Bros
Ralfelson Music

WHITE HEAT* 4:
onna/Pat
Bros

MADONNA

Copyright © 2005 by Essential Works Ltd. All rights reserved.
Printed in China.No part of this book may be used or reproduced
in any manner whatsoever without written permission except in the
case of reprints in the context of reviews. For information, write to
Andrews McMeel Publishing, an Andrews McMeel Universal
company, 4520 Main Street, Kansas City, Missouri 64111.

Library of Congress Cataloging-in-Publication-Data

Madonna : inspirations.
    p. cm.
  ISBN 0-7407-5456-4
  1. Madonna, 1958---Quotations. 2. Madonna, 1958---Portraits

ML420.M1387M219 2005
782.42166'09--dc22

ISBN-13: 978-0-7407-5456-2
ISBN-10: 0-7407-5456-4
Library of Congress Control Number: 2005048000

05 06 07 08 09 IMA 10 9 8 7 6 5 4 3 2 1

Produced by Essential Works
168a Camden Street, London, NW1 9PT, England

Designed by Kate Ward

The publishers have made every reasonable effort to contact
all copyright holders. Any errors that may have occurred are
inadvertent and anyone who for any reason has not been contacted
is invited to write to the publishers so that a full acknowledgment
may be made in subsequent editions of this work.

Attention: Schools and Businesses
Andrews McMeel books are available at quantity discounts with
bulk purchase for educational, business, or sales promotional use.
For information, please write to: Special Sales Department,
Andrews McMeel Publishing, 4520 Main Street, Kansas City,
Missouri 64111.

Madonna photographs
courtesy of Topfoto,
Topfoto/ArenaPal,
Topfoto/Fortean,
Topfoto/Imageworks,
Topfoto/National and
Topfoto/UPP; footprints in
the sand, platform shoes,
nuns, kabbalah courtesy
of Topfoto; office
window courtesy of
Topfoto/National; child's
face, dollar bills courtesy
of Topfoto/Imageworks;
Virgin Mary courtesy of
Topfoto/Fortean; desert
road, thunderstorm, clouds,
peacock, bird of prey,
forest courtesy of
Photodisc; checkered
flag courtesy of Corbis.

Printed in China

MADONNA

inspirations

**Andrews McMeel
Publishing**

Kansas City

WHEN YOUR NAME IS MADONNA

IT'S BEST TO BECOME ONE

I am the
epitome of
the American
dream

I came
from
nothing

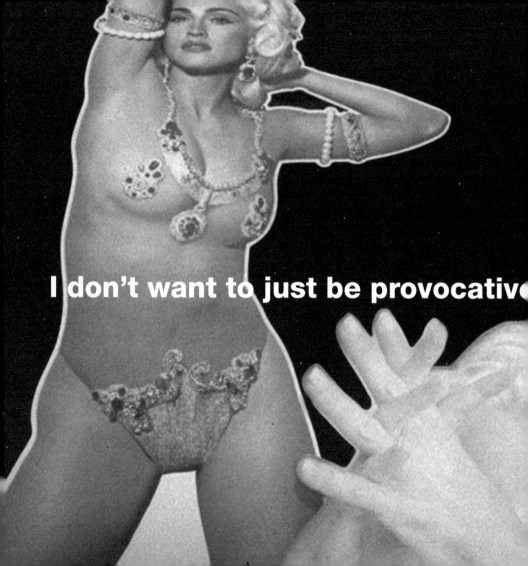

or the sake of being provocative

Way back I
was loud and,
I guess you
could say,
obscene.
Today I use
the power of

(silence)

Everything physical is an illusion . . .

. . . but it's there to guide us

. . . or test us

. . . or deter us.

To be brave is to love someone unconditionally, without expecting anything in return.

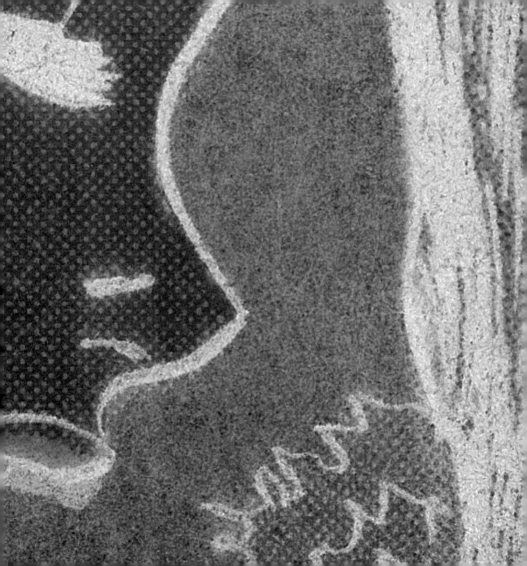

I worry about everything.

I'm really a lot like everybody else.

When in doubt,

act like God.

WE LIVE IN A SOCIETY THAT JUDGES EVERYONE

ON A COMPLETELY SUPERFICIAL LEVEL

it's our nature to only **focus** on a few things in life

How
many
times
have
you
fallen
for
some-
body
just
based
on
how
they
look?

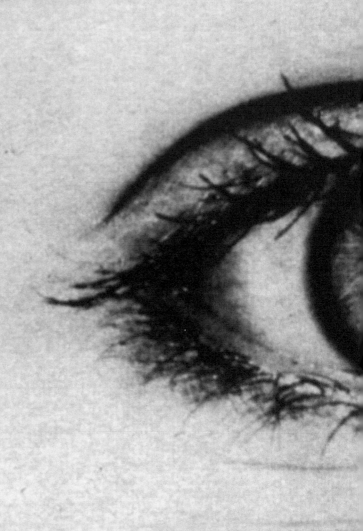

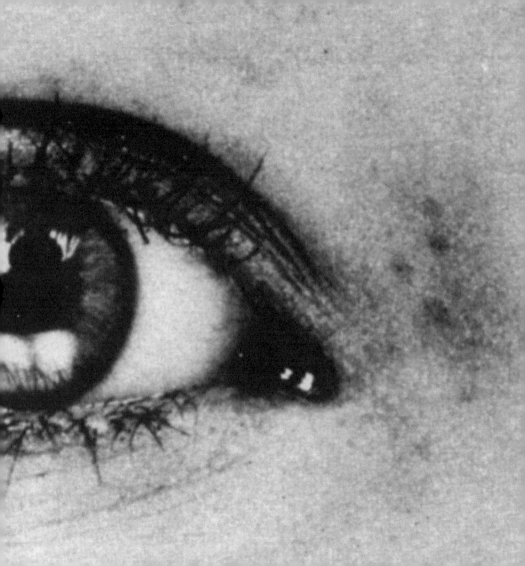

Never forget to dream.

I like knowing that I could figure out a way to live

anywhere

I don't consider myself a

FEMINIST

.

I consider myself a

HUMANIST

I'm not going to cha

ge the world in a day

all of us have God in us

and we have God-like qualities

I'M TOUGH,

I'M AMBITIOUS,

AND I KNOW EXACTLY WHAT I WANT.

IF THAT MAKES ME A BITCH . . .

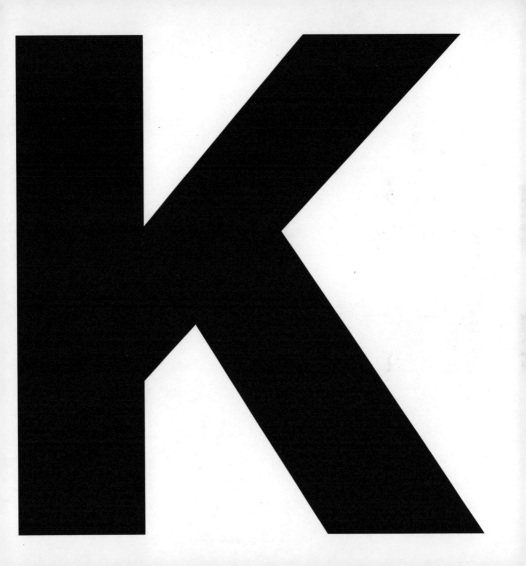

No matter how you try to get away with it, the sin is within you all the time.

People associate a girl who's successful with being a bimbo or an airhead.

Marilyn Monroe

was

a victim

and I'm not

Being loved
keeps
you young

We bring about our own destruction or our own creation

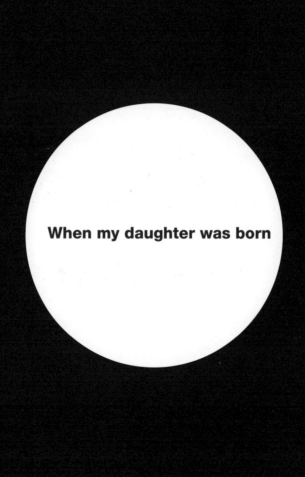

When my daughter was born

I was born again

That pressure

to be beautiful,
to be successful,
to be rich,
to be thin,
to be popular,

it's everyone's pressure.

EVERYBODY PEES IN THE SHOWER

AND EVERYBODY PICKS THEIR NOSE

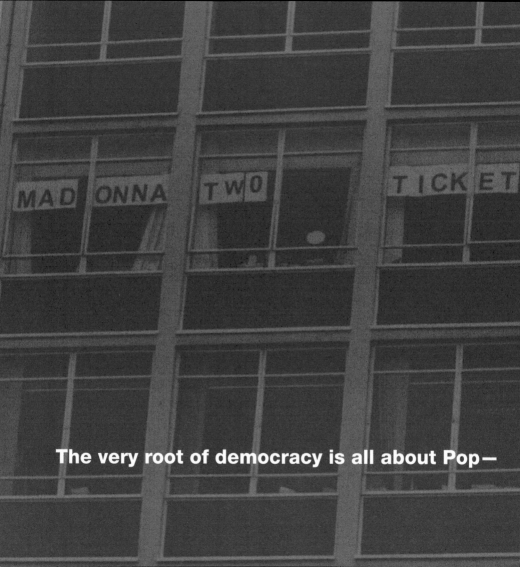

The very root of democracy is all about Pop—

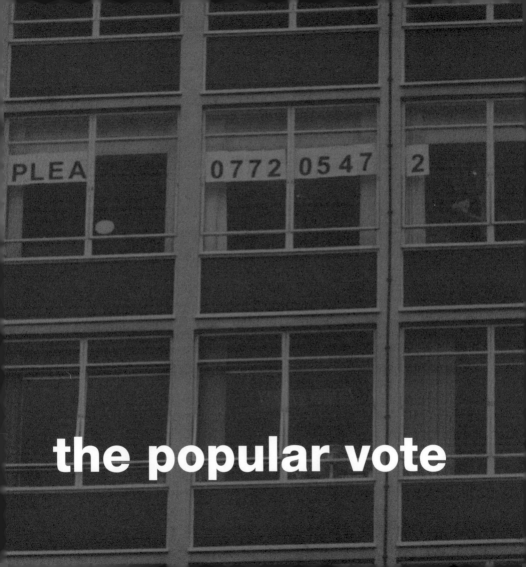

PLEA 0772 0547 2

the popular vote

I've provoked all my life, not for

the sake of creating scandals

or to be political,

but for **my** sake,

my rights as a woman

in a male-dominated society.

Children always understand.

They have open minds.

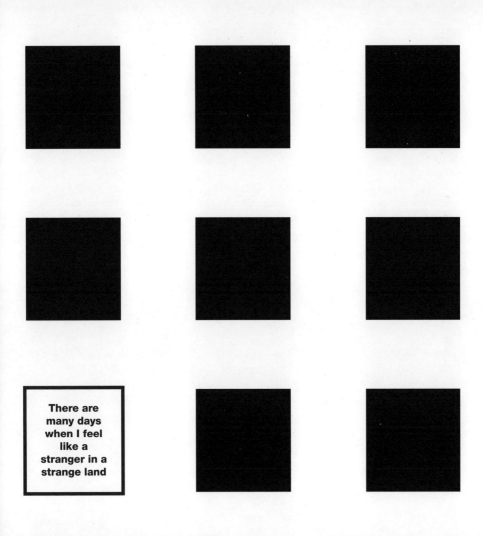

There are
many days
when I feel
like a
stranger in a
strange land

**Catholicism
is
not
a
soothing
religion.
It's a painful religion.
We're
all
gluttons
for
punishment.**

I ACT OUT OF INSTINCT

You have

to be . . .

patient.

[**I'M NOT.**]

You can be sexy

and strong

at the same time

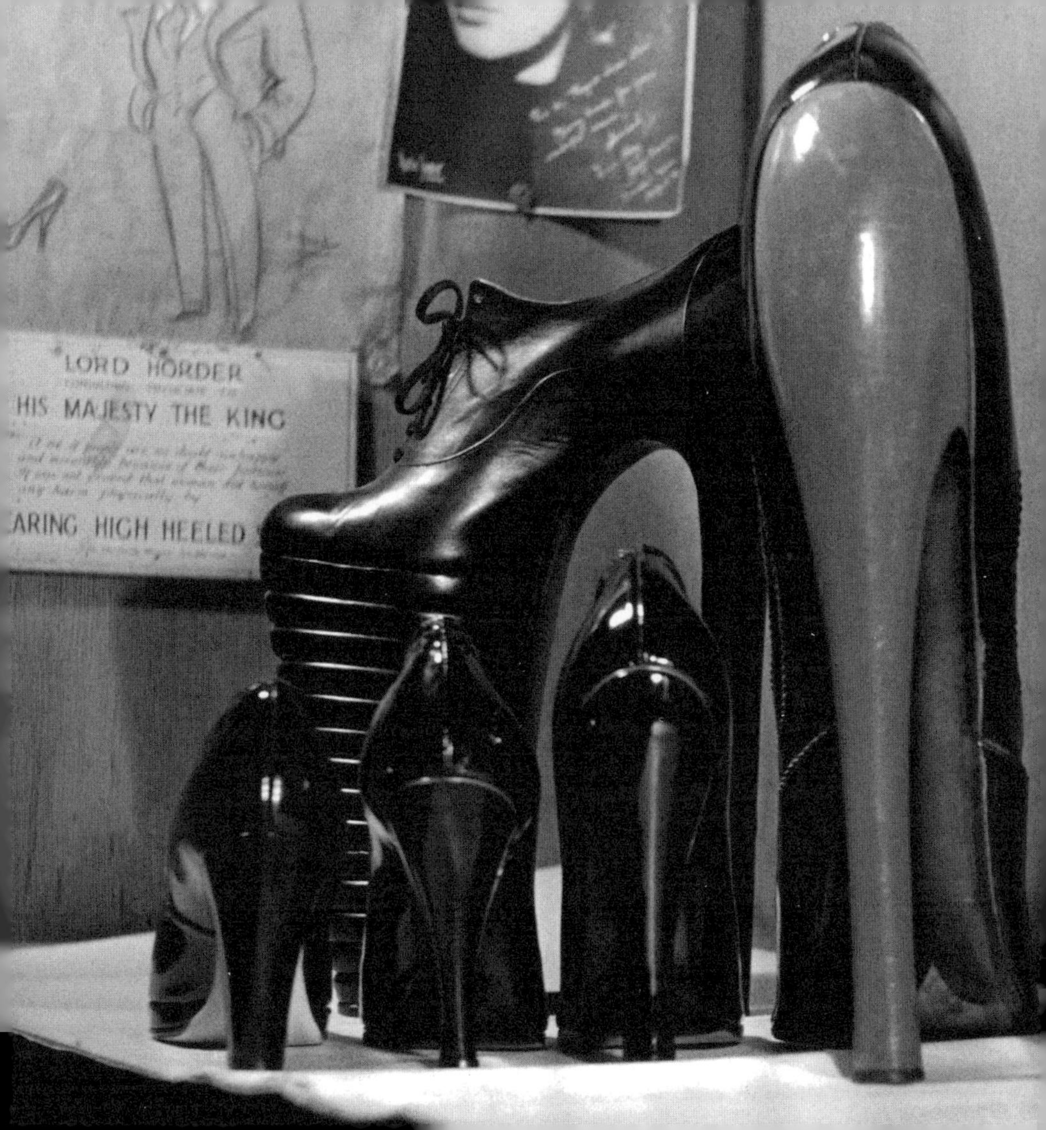
LORD HORDER
HIS MAJESTY THE KING
ARING HIGH HEELED

I always wanted to be **TALLER**

Sometimes I look back at myself and remember things I used to say, or my hairstyle, and I cringe.

I need love.

**Even after I made love
for the first time,
I still felt
I was a
virgin.**

I don't take drugs.

I never did.

I always said I wanted to be famous

I wanted to be . . .

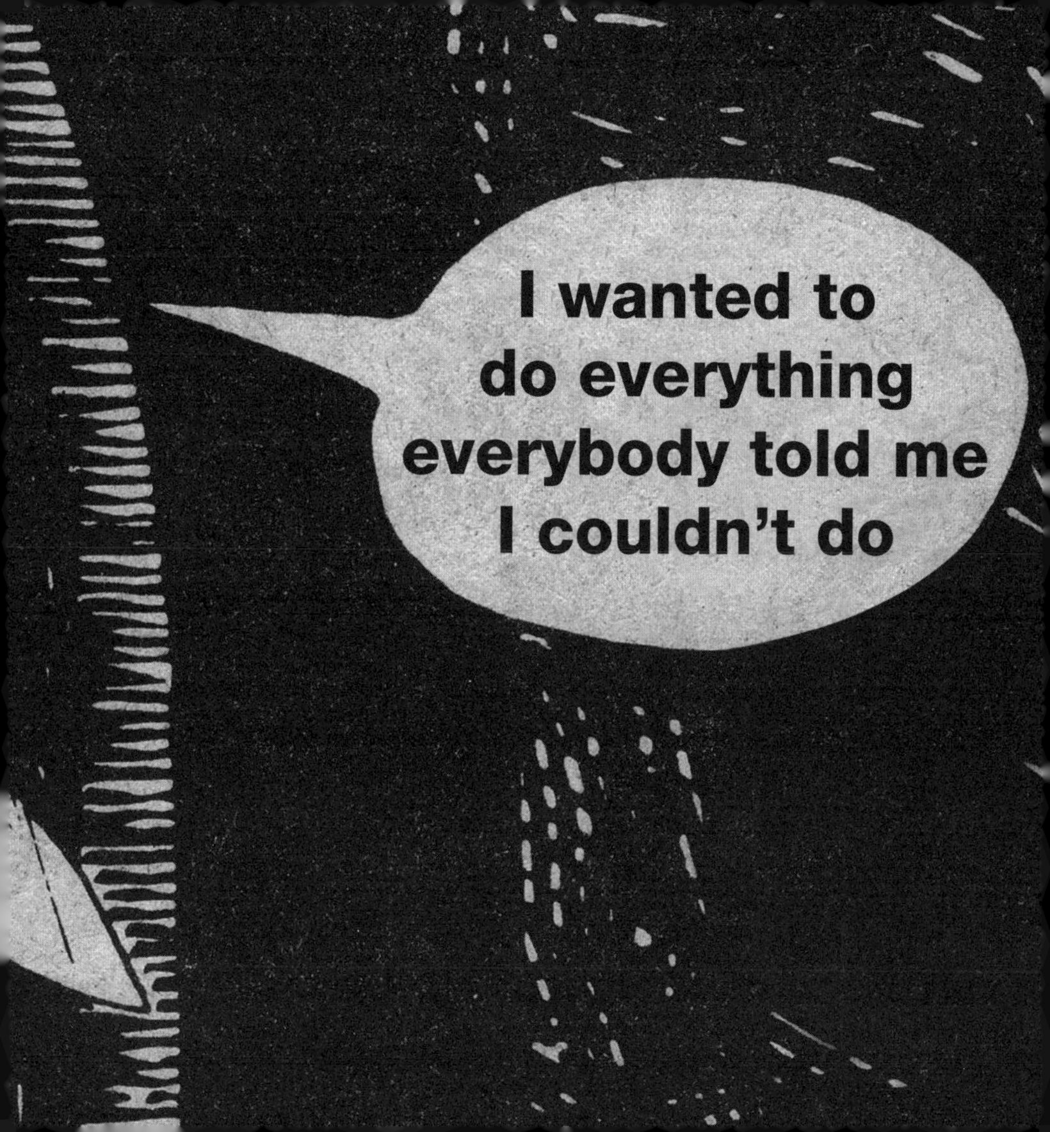
I wanted to do everything everybody told me I couldn't do

extension

my image is a natural

of my performance

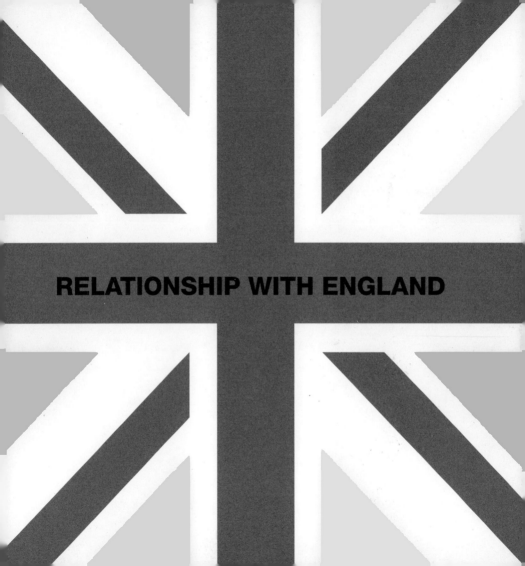

RELATIONSHIP WITH ENGLAND

I am an artist at heart and my heart forces me to keep my eyes open and to try new things,

**but in the past
few years I also learned
how to relax.**

the person who was negative will bring
negativity back towards himself

the person who was negative will bring negativity back towards himself

Romance

should

be

spontaneous

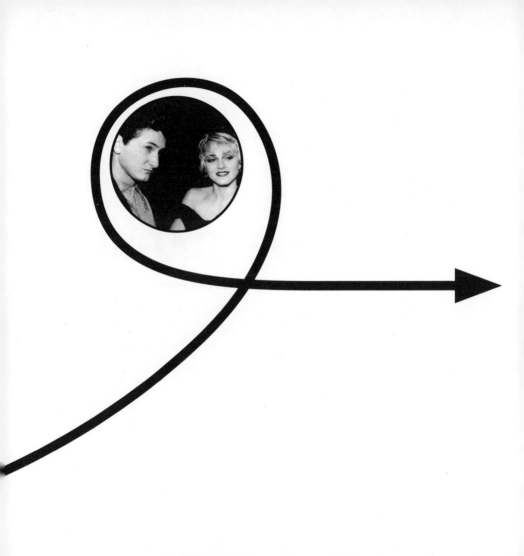

BUT IN MY CAREER

I'M TOTALLY

IN
CONTROL

The older I get, the more I start to
people around and stupidity

ealize that there are a lot of stupid
an make them dangerous

men are quite intimidated by women who accomplish a lot

$$$$$$$$ THE MORE MONEY I MAKE, THE

MORE I CAN HELP OTHER PEOPLE $$$$$$$

Sometimes you have to be a

BITCH

to get things done

WHEN YOU HAVE CHILDREN YOU HAVE TO STEP OUTSIDE OF YOURSELF. YOU CAN'T SIT AROUND FEELING SORRY FOR YOURSELF, OR FEELING LIKE YOU'RE A VICTIM IN ANY WAY, SHAPE, OR FORM.

I wouldn't have turned out

the way I was if I didn't have all those

old-fashioned values

to rebel against

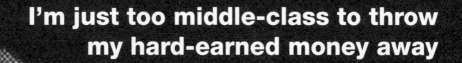

I BELIEVE IN GOD

When I'm hungry,

I eat.

When I'm thirsty,

I drink.

When I feel like

saying something ...

I SA

Y IT.

Americans know how to get things done quicker

I'm at my most creative
when I'm standing at a microphone
and the pressure's on

I'VE NEVER SUCCUMBED TO PEE

PRESSURE

I know that I can do whatever I want and that I'll always reach my goals

It is difficult to believe in a religion that places such a high premium on chastity and virginity

I
have
bigger
plans
and
I
have
more
important
things
to
do

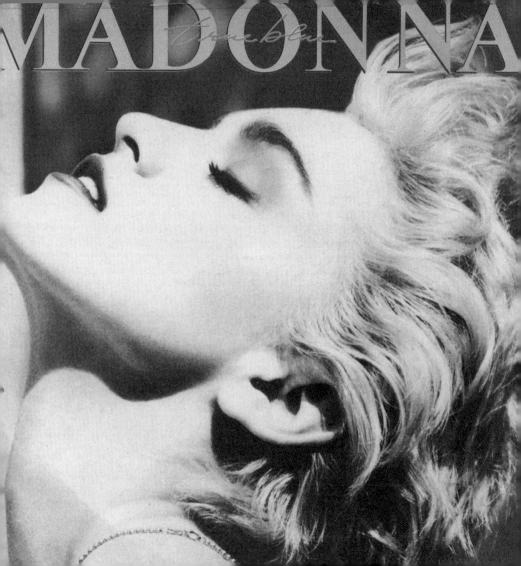

I WANTED TO BE . . .

A NUN

**getting people's approval is
not a goal to have in life**

The worst thing ever written about me was when people were accusing me of having a baby for attention

I'm a mother.

I don't make
plans anymore.

That's future
enough for me.

The rest will
happen by itself.

**I'm a very
old-fashioned
girl.**

STUDYING KABBALAH IS A VERY CHALLENGING THING TO DO. IT REQUIRES A LOT OF WORK, A LOT OF READING, A LOT OF TIME, A LOT OF COMMITMENT, AND A LOT OF DISCIPLINE.

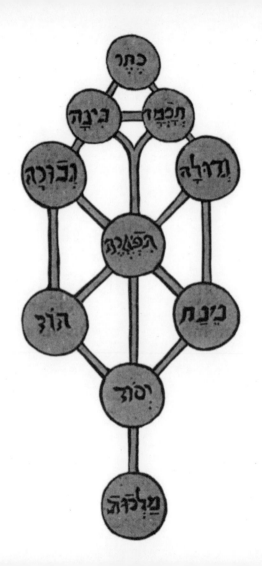

I've been . . .

popular a

successful

loved a

unpopular

unsuccessful

loathed

. . . and I know how meaningless it all is